Feeling well within

A GUIDE TO TURNING INTO THE PARENT YOU DESIRE

Carol C. Smith

Table of Contents

Introduction

This is a thorough and perceptive book that provides parents who want to raise their children in a loving and rewarding atmosphere with expert counsel, helpful tips, and insightful information.

This book examines many facets of parenting and gives readers a road map for navigating the difficulties and rewards of being a parent. It does this by relying on in-depth research and the knowledge of top parenting authorities. Regardless of your level of parenting experience, this book will equip you with the skills and information you need to be the kind of parent you want to be. The first chapter of the book explores the significance of self-awareness and self-care for parents. It highlights how important it is to comprehend one's own values, beliefs, and emotions to develop a constructive parenting style. Readers are encouraged to examine their own parenting styles and pinpoint areas in which they need to improve through useful exercises and thought-provoking questions. Important subjects, including effective communication, establishing boundaries, developing emotional intelligence, encouraging good behaviors, and building resilience in kids,

Readers will discover how to develop stronger bonds with their kids while supporting their emotional well-being, from mindful discipline to attentive listening.These professional viewpoints give parents a better knowledge of how children develop as well as helpful advice for dealing with certain difficulties that may come up. It further acknowledges that each child is unique and exhorts parents to value their uniqueness while creating a nurturing atmosphere for their development. It underlines how crucial it is to promote inclusivity in families and celebrate variety.

This is a helpful tool for parents looking to establish a loving and peaceful home environment because it is written in an interesting and approachable manner. The book is a vital resource for parents who wish to raise self-assured, resilient, and compassionate kids because of its relevant anecdotes, useful activities, and evidence-based tactics.

It provides you with the knowledge and resources you need to create a loving and rewarding parenting journey, regardless of whether you are navigating the early years of parenthood or dealing with the difficulties of adolescence. Build a balanced family life that brings out the best in you and your kids, and find your inner strength as a parent.

Chapter 1
Positive Inside: The Value of Introspection and Self-Care

It's critical to realize that raising children is only one facet of our lives; leading a holistically healthy life involves many more facets as well. We cannot sacrifice those aspects of our lives in an attempt to achieve instant perfection. After realizing this, every mother would agree that, in addition to her many other responsibilities, such as raising her children, she also has some self-care obligations. We refer to this as "self-responsibility."
As individuals, we should ideally not feel guilty or selfish for prioritizing our own needs. Instead, we should owe it to ourselves first. We won't be able to care for others if we don't first take care of ourselves. Therefore, it's critical to set aside some guilt-free time each day for activities that help us unwind or feel good about

ourselves.   Parent-child relationships are invariably characterized by a "mirroring effect. Children are sensitive to their early experiences in life and are also intelligent learners. Instinctively, they see their parents as role models. This information should increase our awareness since it affects not just ourselves but also everyone close to us, especially our kids when we neglect our own needs.

Self-sufficient parents are more likely to be approachable and capable of attending to their kids' needs. They show their own children the same level of care because of their abilities and dedication to their own physical and emotional well-being. Because we need to set a healthy example for our kids. Self-care demonstrates to kids that we take care of ourselves, which helps them learn how to take care of themselves. To meet the demands of life, including restorative self-care practices, our children must acquire coping and problem-solving abilities.

When it comes to parenting, it's acceptable to feel uncertain and even afraid. We battle not just the rapid changes and demands of today's society but also our own unsolved problems and fears. Every stage of parenthood brings with it fresh challenges and issues, sometimes serving as a reminder of how we view our own youth. We might have doubts and queries, some based on experience and logic, others grounded in uncertainty, but all causing worry and discomfort.

Even with a great deal of introspection, we could find it difficult to accept the different obstacles in life and our intrinsic duty to prioritize our kids. However, because it is closely related to how we interpret our own early experiences, how we see ourselves in this role is crucial. This, in turn, has an impact on our parenting style.

Neither the only nor the most significant factors relating to this job are doubts, worries, or insecurities. Every one of them is eclipsed by opportunity! Every day, as we are pushed back toward a close parent-child bond, parents and guardians are allowed to develop personally.

In the end, having us is advantageous to our kids. Only we can provide the compassionate understanding that we may have yearned for as kids—an understanding that will undoubtedly be helpful to our kids.

In fact, we shouldn't ignore or deny the same struggles we may have had as kids in the past. We must make meaning of those difficult experiences if we are to digest them, comprehend them, and keep from projecting and repeating the same unfavorable relationships with our own children.

But that doesn't mean we have to sacrifice ourselves or our wants to be the greatest parents we can be for our kids.It's acceptable to make errors. We must continuously remind ourselves that maturation, experience, and time all contribute to our personal development. Making errors is OK since they provide chances for improvement. None of the babies ever came out with a manual, after all.

We must strive for traits rather than ones that we are born with. As parents or guardians, we can break away from old patterns that bind us to the present by helping us make sense of life. Gaining self-awareness might enable us to cultivate more fulfilling and productive relationships with others around us—something we certainly deserve. In addition to active play, listening, guiding, and love, our role as parents includes responsibility to take care of ourselves.

Doubts, unanswered questions, and past problems do not go away when we become parents. If they are not understood and processed, they not only persist but also get stronger. This serves as even more justification for taking proactive rather than reactive steps to take care of ourselves and our needs. This has a significant impact on both our relationship with ourselves and our inner child, as well as the relationships we have with the people we love and how they are regarded.

First, fill your cup. By putting your well-being first, you may manage the energy required for excellent parenting by maintaining concentration on your career and other responsibilities. Your children will learn the value of self-care when they observe you scheduling time for it, Consider it. How can you be a good parent if you don't get enough sleep? How can you have the energy to be a great parent and complete your vital work at the same time if you don't consume a nutritious diet?

If we stop practicing self-care, exercising, and maintaining healthy habits and use time constraints as an excuse, we risk developing stress, overwhelm, and anxiety. It's your time now. How can you take better care of yourself at home?

Get up early to meditate before the children arrive.

Make use of visualization techniques to see a successful and motivating day ahead of you.

Write in your journal to get all of your ideas and worries out of your head and onto paper.

Make a note of everything for which you are thankful, and concentrate on the positive aspects of each day.To help you cope with being overwhelmed, list your top three to four priorities every morning.

Make the choice to prioritize eating wholesome, fresh foods for optimal energy.
Try not to use your smartphone too much if you want to feel less overwhelmed, stressed, and exhausted.
  Pay attention to one item at a time, and keep in mind that multitasking uses up energy.
To be well hydrated, drink 1.5 liters of water per day.Even if all you do is jog around the block, try to get in 30 minutes of activity every day. Well, read this twice before you leave: taking care of yourself is not selfish. Quite the contrary—it's among the greatest presents you can offer your kids and yourself. Yes, especially in these trying times, stepping back from your parental responsibilities can cause shame and anxiety. However, taking that much-needed break makes you happier, healthier, more patient, and gives you more energy.

Chapter 2
Early childhood education is important for good communication.

The main goal of parenting is to communicate with your child. Fostering healthy bidirectional communication is crucial to your child's development of self-worth. Even though words of support and affirmation are often beneficial to children, listening to them helps them feel valued and loved. It's important to keep in mind that kids can comprehend language long before they can speak. By giving your child your undivided attention every day, you can stay on top of their changing language development.

You are laying the groundwork for future positive habits when you establish open and transparent communication channels with your child in their early years.
Goodwill interactions with small children
Early childhood experiences have a big impact on a child's subsequent self-motivation, stress management, and sense of confidence. A person's perception of themselves and their position in their family and community is their "self-concept.

Establishing a healthy self-concept in a child is mostly dependent on the quality of the relationships between parents and children. A youngster who experiences continual criticism, judgment, and blame may have a poor self-concept as an adult. Pay attention to your kids. Be sure you set a good example for your child if you want them to learn how to listen well. Give them your full attention. It makes sense that parents who are constantly busy and preoccupied would occasionally choose to ignore a noisy child. However, if you neglect your child all the time, it conveys that you don't value their opinions and that you don't listen to them.

Whenever you can, listen intently to what your youngster has to say. If your schedule is hectic, make sure to set aside some time each day to just sit and listen to your child. Encourage the thoughts and opinions of your child. Both sides must listen and talk in turn for there to be effective communication.

Instead of focusing on fixing their grammar or finishing their sentences, attempt to understand what they are trying to express.

Talk about difficult or significant topics without worrying about being overly defensive, criticized, or placed at fault.

Probably one of the most rewarding and challenging occupations in the world is raising a child. Our world is fast-paced and full of complicated issues that are difficult for most parents to convey to their children and for most children to understand. Sometimes parents don't realize how much this complexity causes difficulty for their kids. Without appropriate direction, kids are more likely to make bad decisions based more on peer pressure than good reasoning. To help kids traverse this complexity and develop a sound grasp of the world around them, effective communication can go a long way.

The majority of parents do not understand the value of spending time with their children in person, listening, and conversing. Some of those who do lament that they don't have enough time. Many parents undervalue the significance of their children's emotional and psychological well-being because they believe that giving their kids a healthy environment and nourishing food is enough to ensure their well-being.

Parental participation in a child's growth is crucial, according to numerous studies. Being an engaged listener is essential for parents to learn to communicate effectively.

Children require ongoing care and attention from the moment they are born. They tend to become more independent as they get older. They do, however, require the emotional stability that comes with adult assistance while they travel this path. To give young children the emotional support they require to feel significant and valued, communication is essential. Children benefit greatly from spending time with their parents in numerous ways, including developing the guts and confidence to confront the outside world. Since children learn best through observation, this allows them to acquire socialization, bonding, and connection qualities, as well as the value of friendship. By talking and listening to them, parents may help their children develop positive relationships with one another and foster an environment where they feel comfortable sharing their needs, worries, wants, likes, dislikes, emotions, and other issues.

In addition, it provides them with the comfort of knowing that help is always available.

Setting aside time for their children can be challenging for working parents. Simple tactics that might not call for an official face-to-face talk might be an alternative when time is of the essence. One quick and simple way to remain in touch is to give them a call and have a conversation.

Encouraging kids to do things like draw would be enjoyable for them and aid in their ability to communicate their emotions and ideas. Asking a child to sketch a picture of her playground is one example. Parents can use this to observe the child's positioning as well as basic information about her classmates, teachers, and favorite games. Some kids will express themselves more during activities than during a face-to-face discussion with a parent.

Another choice would be to talk to each other in the car on the way to and from school, during grocery shopping, on walks in the evening, at supper, or even right before bed. Not every child will be willing to chat, so for parents who can find time to talk to their kids, it's critical to make every encounter unique. Making these gatherings unique facilitates connection. Baking, gardening, and working on crafts involving clay or other materials could potentially be used to accomplish this.

Asking them to talk about themselves is another good topic; this helps them recognize and comprehend who they are.

It encourages the assessment of actions, sentiments, emotions, and individual thoughts and perspectives. It also allows kids to discover their own talents and interests. Asking them about their thoughts and opinions regarding particular cultural and personal elements enables them to discuss what they enjoy and dislike about themselves and their own culture, as well as how they fit in. Talking about spirituality would be acceptable as well. To assist their children in creating their own perspectives and interests and to help them understand how things function, parents could share some of their own personal experiences and anecdotes. Parents should constantly serve as positive role models for their children, helping them learn and improve in whatever they do.

Advantages of listening and speaking

Good communication is very beneficial to the parents as well as the kids. This helps parents better grasp the characters of their kids. It keeps their connection strong and based on love and trust while allowing them to connect. The parent-child bond is strengthened, and both parties' burden of suppressing their feelings is lessened when they communicate and listen to one another.

Children learn to be attached to and committed to their families. This prevents individuals from becoming lost in society and engaging in bad habits, such as drug abuse, gang membership, other antisocial behavior, or unsafe sexual activity. Children are more willing to disclose information about their peers and their involvement levels when parents and they communicate well, which facilitates parents' attentive supervision of their children.   Additionally, it enables kids to talk about issues they might be having in relationships or friendships and helps them resolve them more successfully.

When parents don't talk to their kids about these things, the kids feel more at ease talking to their friends about it, and those friends typically steer the kids toward drug usage or other abusive behaviors. These buddies prey on troubled individuals by convincing them to engage in dangerous sexual activities or by raping them while they are under the influence of drugs or alcohol. Because they are stressed and anxious about handling and solving a situation on their own, children also begin to develop a variety of psychological and physical issues. Helping kids find solutions to their issues promotes emotional development and maturity in them.

Chapter 3
Adaptability above happiness

Negative emotions stand in the way of happiness as a goal, every one of us has a right to our own emotions. The good-inside parenting philosophy never suggests avoiding, judging, or changing a child's feeling, you do want the best for your kids. However, avoiding conflicts, not believing in your own emotions, and feeling "bad" about your lack of happiness can all contribute to anxiety in the future. Resiliency is a much better objective to concentrate on. A Resilient youngster can control their responses, comprehend and believe in their feelings, and feel confident in their own skin. Achieving the desired result is not the goal of resilience. Recall that your role is to enforce rules, not to manage your child's emotions. It's OK to have to endure the tantrum for a while. Some skills, such as empathy, presence, acceptance, and listening, are necessary while

teaching resilience. Your youngster
has to be able to recognize their
talents and develop independent
problem-solving skills.

The difficult part is that to
achieve your goals for your child,
you must also show yourself the
same respect and love. Because of
this, teaching kids to have a
connection-based worldview also
involves improving oneself.
Because our relationship with
ourselves will always be the
foundation of our relationships with
everyone else, including our
children.To achieve resilience, you
must not only improve yourself but
also recognize conduct as an insight
into your child's inner reality.
Remember to use your most
understanding interpretation,
acknowledge that two things are
true, and approach the situation
with an open mind whenever
shocking behaviors arise. Parents
frequently place too much emphasis
on their children's pleasure because
they only want what is best for
them. However, resilience—which
aids kids in controlling challenging
emotions and stressful
circumstances—is the precursor to

happiness. Being resilient is not a set quality.

It's a talent that parents can foster in their kids.Not a single parent that I know of doesn't want the best for their children. I'm in! I want what's best for my children! However, I don't think that "the best" for kids is to "just be happy . After all, controlling distress is necessary to cultivate happiness. Before we can feel content, we must feel protected. Why is it that we must first learn how to control the difficult stuff? Why is happiness unable to just "win" and "beat" all other feelings? That would undoubtedly be simpler! It's unfortunate that the most important things in life, including parenting,require effort and time. Supporting your child in developing resilience isn't simple, but it will be worthwhile, I assure you.
Although stress and hardship are inherent aspects of life, developing resilience doesn't make us immune to them; rather, it affects how we respond to and experience those trying times. Resilient people are better equipped to handle tough situations. Here's a useful (if a little

simplistic) formula: Internal experience equals stress and coping. The favorable tidings? Resilience is a talent that can be developed and is something that, ideally, parents should implant in their children from an early age. It is not a fixed character characteristic that children either possess or lack. Since we are unable to always alter the stressors in our environment, we can always improve our capacity for resilience. Connecting with our "inner parent," the place where our innate capacity to parent and our natural love for our child collide, is essential to developing parental emotional resilience. Investing in our parental self-awareness—that is, knowing and understanding ourselves as parents—while keeping in mind that parenting is a voyage of discovery on which we discover new things about our child daily, is crucial to this.

Unconditional love and acceptance of our child's uniqueness are equally important. Being joyful and feeling good about ourselves is essential to our emotional resilience as parents. It goes without saying that unless we are raising our children in a safe and secure atmosphere, parental emotional resilience cannot flourish. Building resilience takes work, but it's work that benefits our kids as well as ourselves. One of the most crucial things we will do is raise resilient and emotionally healthy children. Our child has the best opportunity to enjoy childhood and develop into a happy, successful adult when they are in good emotional health. Most likely, they are the ones who will raise emotionally stable kids of their own.

The inability of a child to manage common emotions like envy, disappointment, frustration, and melancholy will impede their capacity to develop happiness. On the other hand, children can acquire the mental calmness required for happiness if we teach them how to control their emotions.It is comparable to the proverb that states, "Give a man a fish, and he will eat for a day."Putting a bandage over the problem is what happens when we focus on

happiness instead of the underlying conditions that create it."
Resilience is far more enticing, in my opinion than happiness, since achieving happiness requires controlling distress. Before we can feel content, we must feel protected. Why is it that we must first learn how to control the difficult stuff? Why is happiness unable to just "win" and "beat" all other feelings? That would undoubtedly be simpler! Every night before bed, parents should have a 10-minute conversation with their children to help them develop resilience. We should ask them if they have any problems at school or with friends if they are angry with us, or if they are worried about anything. Parents should also listen to their children's accounts of their day without passing judgment and reassure them that they have experienced similar things themselves.

Children can learn that everyone faces difficulties and how to put their disappointments in perspective by participating in this parent-child conversation. Parents should hopefully help instill resilience in their children from an early age, resilience is not a static character trait that children either possess or lack. While we can't always control the stressors in our environment, we can always work on developing our capacity for resilience.

Chapter 4
Connection is essential

Even though we instinctively know how important it is to connect with our children, we frequently overlook it when life gets hectic. The bond that our children have with us is ultimately what matters most. The benefits of spending time bonding with our children are numerous.

The most effective method of discipline for our kids is to have a close relationship with them. Power struggles are the least effective technique to get them to listen. Children care about the things that matter to us when they feel a connection to us. They take our instructions with gusto.

Your child's behavior and your connection will both be greatly improved if you connect with them instead of reprimanding them.

Developing relationships takes time. This is not a case of fixing it and forgetting it. It's necessary to build, nurture, and maintain relationships.

Deliberate one-on-one time spent away from your phone is one way you can do that. It's not necessary to give up displays for a week or turn off your internet. Just make it a point to set aside regular times when you put your phone away and give your kids your full attention.

A technique to build connections with kids before significant events is through emotional immunization. Perhaps you sit down with your child and discuss what's going to happen before the first day of school. Recognize any emotions or worries you may have. Tell a tale of a comparable encounter you had.

Emotions are not the issue. The issue is feeling isolated in one's emotions. The "feeling bench" represents a child's emotional state during a significant event that they are unable to comprehend.

Sometimes all that's required is to simply sit with them on the bench and let them know they're safe and not alone.

Reflection, acknowledgment, sharing what you would do differently, and connecting with inquiry and understanding are the four essential elements in the healing process.

Although it fosters the ideal setting for children to manifest their inner goodness, connection-building is a continuous process that does not eliminate undesirable behaviors. Let's discuss negative habits in the next part, followed by typical actions that appear terrible.

Express your love. Yes, every stage of life requires a human touch and genuine affection for healthy neurological and emotional development. You must give your child hugs and other tender touches multiple times during the day. Consider each exchange as a chance to build a relationship with your child. Make sure to smile, make eye contact, greet them warmly, and promote open communication. Repeat "I love you" a lot.

Although it's frequently assumed that we love our kids, regardless of their age, make sure to tell them every day.A simple "I love you" can make a big difference in your relationship with your child in the long run. Establish limits, guidelines, and sanctions.

As they mature and gain knowledge of their surroundings, children require direction and structure. Make sure your kids understand what you expect of them by having a conversation with them about it. Make sure age-appropriate sanctions are in place and that you consistently enforce them when rules are breached.

Pay attention and show compassion.

Listening is the first step towards connection.You teach your youngster respect for others by listening to them and showing empathy.

Engage in play together.

Play is crucial for a child's growth. Children use it as a tool to enhance their language abilities, communicate their feelings, encourage creativity, and pick up social skills.No matter what you play, it does not matter. Simply enjoying each other and resolving to give your child your full attention is crucial.

Be accessible and free from interruptions. A small daily commitment of 10 uninterrupted minutes can go a long way toward helping your child develop positive communication skills.

Share meals with one another.Urge everyone to just enjoy each other's company by putting aside their phones and other electronics. You may also use mealtimes to educate your kids on the value of eating a balanced, healthy diet, which has a positive impact on their general mental health.

Establish routines between parents and children. Spending quality time with your child one-on-one can improve their sense of self-worth, the parent-child relationship, and their sense of uniqueness and value. To generate that one-on-one time, some parents plan special "date nights" with their kids. It's crucial to honor each child individually; it can be as simple as watching a movie at home or going for a walk around the neighborhood or to the playground.

Chapter 5
"Is it too late to change the way I parent my child— and will it actually work if I do?"

This is a common question that parents ask Empowering Parents in their correspondence. How to modify your parenting style in this book greatly increases the likelihood that your child's behavior will improve.

Focus on the behavior you wish to alter the most before moving on to the next. Avoid attempting to do everything at once.

Some parents worry that no matter what they do, their child won't change. Many find that when their child misbehaves, they quickly react, yelling and screaming or becoming entangled in power conflicts as soon as the youngster acts out. Parents can easily become disheartened even when they do something new. Some occasionally attempt to try new approaches but finally give up when these don't appear to work. This is particularly true if they have been unable to address the behavior for years and it has become a problem.

You frequently end up just reacting to what your children do rather than responding properly if you don't truly take the time to consider your reaction.

Many parents get upset with their child's actions and want to discipline them right away. Regrettably, the child receives no useful training from doing this; in the end, it is ineffective. The terms "react"and "respond"have rather different meanings. Reacting is more akin to a reflex; your buttons are pressed, and you go into your routine. However, you're being more impartial if you're answering. While you will still hold your child accountable, you will have more time to think through the punishment and the lesson you want him to learn. Additionally, there is a decreased likelihood that you will become emotionally attached to your child's actions.

Although it might not always be simple, there are practical things you can do immediately to alter the way you react and help your child behave better. These are seven strategies to begin raising your child more skillfully.

1.Select the task you want to work on initially. One issue I observe with parents is that they are unsure of where to begin. However, I believe it's quite easy: begin with the items that endanger your child. These are the actions that put your child or others in danger, whether they be through physical harm, property destruction, or danger when they are not at home. Free Personal Parenting Plan Offer for Empowering Parents I can assure you that you will be disappointed if you expect to make all the changes at once. That's not only not feasible, but you'll drive your child away as well. In my opinion, parents ought to confront matters that go against their beliefs and values and pose a danger to their children as well as others. Do we wish to make all the changes? Good luck; perhaps we can. However, I believe that we should begin with the riskiest and most dangerous things first and then proceed.

2. Identify the specific things you wish to change. it's beneficial for parents to dissect behaviors into manageable chunks and address each one separately. Thus, begin with the behavior you wish to modify the most if your child screams at you, storms up to his room, and slams the door. You want to dissect it when you speak with him. Say this first: "Don't swear. That offends me and doesn't help to fix the issue. When you're upset, what would you do differently, in your opinion? Even when your child isn't able to think of anything, give him some ideas and ask him to select one. Thus, focus on the behavior you wish to alter the most before moving on to the next.

3. Avoid attempting to do everything at once. Describe the modification. It could be beneficial to have a conversation with your child about the changes you plan to make if you're going to modify a particular response to a behavior.

You can say something like, "Oh, by the way, I wanted to tell you something," when everything is going smoothly and everyone is at ease. I don't think it works around here to have you grounded in your room all day when you use foul language. You don't seem to be changing as a result of it.

You will thus have to stay in your room until you compose an apology letter if you use profanity. After you've finished reading that letter, you can read it aloud to me, and we can discuss it. To ensure you stay on course, I'm going to take away your phone and computer while you're in your room. Even though your child may become irritated, try not to allow him to start a fight. you may say, I advise you to avoid giving speeches and instead to make brief, targeted observations. Recall that speeches reduce the amount of communication.

4. Specify your objective. Clearly stating your objectives to your youngster is crucial, in my opinion.My goal is that you don't throw sand in kids' faces or bite them when they're playing in the sandbox. So let's work together to find an alternative approach for you to take going forward to avoid any problems. What else can you do when someone makes fun of you? and devise a strategy for what he might do in the future.

It's critical to acknowledge that your words may not always reach your child's ears in the manner you would like. Thus, attempt to maintain your composure even if your youngster seems bewildered by you during your conversation. He may also be worried, upset, or disappointed.

However, it's a method of handling issues that will eventually alter his views of his relationship with you and with authority.

5. Manage Opportunity If you're concerned that your child is going to do something unpleasant or damaging, one of your alternatives is to manage the possibilities he has. Let's imagine you have a teenager who continually gets speeding fines. Your attempts to persuade him to accept responsibility and drive more cautiously are met with silence. Removing his car is one of the things you can do. You are denying yourself the chance when you act in that way. It's the same with younger children.

Put a lock on your door or place your pocketbook in the trunk of your car to take away their ability to steal money from your wallet if they continue to do so.

Managing opportunities is one of the easiest methods to influence behavior. Put another way, don't take your daughter to the mall if she can't manage it without having tantrums. Take your son out of the restaurant if he is behaving badly while he is there. As soon as your child shows you that he is incapable of handling something, take away the opportunity until he proves to you otherwise. If your youngster isn't given the chance to do something, it won't happen very often.

6. Avoid using your child's empathy

However, youngsters lack empathy for anyone, and teenagers in particular. They just aren't aware of such emotions. Some claim that the mental machinery responsible for regulating empathy is still developing and not fully functional.

Whatever the reason, you cannot persuade your child of anything by showing empathy. As such, they lack empathy for commonplace circumstances; thus, you cannot rely on that strategy to modify their conduct. You must instead act in their best interests. Show your child that making the adjustment is in his best interests and that it will benefit him in the long run if you want him to change.

You must present the situation in a way that helps your child see the advantages of quitting lying or manipulating. keep in mind that the consequences won't end until the manipulation does. So quit torturing yourself in this way.

7. Define boundaries and impose penalties.

I believe that teaching our children how to set boundaries However, we may, in a sense, make them thirsty for change if we utilize the correct mix of incentives and consequences. Recall that penalties are just a tool. And keep using it if you discover a result that works well. Daries is a crucial part of raising them.

Always keep a larger hammer in your kit, but go gradually.

The truth is, your child will change at some point, if not for you, then for his supervisor, a judge, a probation officer, or a lover. Hopefully, he'll come to his senses before committing too much self-harm. How can you determine whether to alter your parenting approach, then? If the parenting style you have been using has not worked, then I think you need to make a change. There is advice on how to be a good parent, how to discipline your child well, and how to have constructive dialogue with your child that doesn't lead to justifications.

Conclusion

The core values of the Feeling well inside approach to child rearing are love and respect. The majority of the behaviors exhibited by children should be readily comprehensible. After all, even as adults, we still exhibit many of those same habits. Understand that altering conduct isn't the main solution and that behavior itself isn't the issue.

Your child has good morals. They are acting in this manner for a reason. You have to establish a connection before you can address their behavior. It's your responsibility to set limits. Additionally, by carrying out these actions, you're fostering an atmosphere that makes your youngsters feel good about themselves and protected. The importance of parenting cannot be overstated. It determines whether a child grows up to be a productive member of society. Children who receive the right kind of affection and support grow more quickly and acquire a good attitude toward life and its challenges.

A well-raised child learns how to navigate life's obstacles and what to expect from them. No parent should ever wish for their child to seek guidance or assistance from someone else. Regardless of age, parents' top focus should always be raising their children.

A child requires consistent guidance, effective communication, and supervision when following regulations. The bond between a parent and child is very important as it molds the child's character, life choices, and overall behavior. Their emotional, mental, physical, and social wellbeing could also be affected. Children who have positive relationships with their parents are more likely to become well-liked Adults.